little Miss Wise

by Roger Hargreaves

Little Miss Wise was as wise as an owl.

Possibly two owls.

Being so wise and sensible meant
that Little Miss Wise
brushed her teeth every day,
made her bed every day,
tidied her house every day,
and did lots of other
wise and sensible things.

If you are as wise as Little Miss Wise,
you'll know just what kind of other things she did.

Little Miss Wise liked to go for a walk
every day.

A walk that was neither too long, nor too short.

A walk that was wise and sensible.

Or sensible and wise, if you prefer.

On her walks she often met other people.

People who were not quite so wise.

And sometimes, people who were decidely unwise.

Last Monday she met Little Miss Naughty.

"Come and jump in the puddles!"
cried Little Miss Naughty,
with a naughty gleam in her eye.

But Little Miss Wise,
being wise,
refused.

She didn't want to get HER feet wet.

On Tuesday she met Little Miss Greedy,
who was carrying an enormous cake filled
with cream and smothered with pink icing.

"Would you like some of this?"
asked Little Miss Greedy.

Little Miss Wise refused.

She didn't want an upset stomach.

On Wednesday Little Miss Wise refused to get into Mr Busy's racing car.

She didn't want to have an accident.

On Thursday she refused to go into
Mr Messy's house.

"If I go into his house I will get dirty,"
she said to herself.

But she didn't say anything to Mr Messy.

She didn't want to hurt his feelings.

On Friday she refused to
play tennis with Mr Silly.

There's nothing silly about that,
is there?

By Saturday, Little Miss Wise was feeling unhappy.

"If I keep saying 'no' all the time, I'll upset everybody and I won't have any friends left," she said to herself.

She thought long and hard about the problem, and being the wise and sensible person she is, she came up with an answer.

"From now on, I will say 'yes' to everything."

On Sunday, while she was out on one of her
wise and sensible walks, or sensible and wise
walks, if you prefer, Little Miss Wise met Mr Mischief.

He was carrying a parcel.

"Please accept this small present," he said to her.

"N..." began Little Miss Wise.
but then she remembered her decision.

"Yes! Thank you!" she cried.

She took the parcel.

And off skipped Mr Mischief
with a mischievous grin on his face.

Little Miss Wise opened the parcel.

"ATISHOO!" she sneezed.

Then she sneezed again.

And she sneezed, and sneezed, and sneezed
all day long.

She used 199 handkerchiefs.

Mr Mischief's present
had been sneezing powder!

Today is Monday and Little Miss Wise
has stopped sneezing.

She is on one of her wise and sensible walks,
or sensible and wise walks, if you prefer,
and she has met Mr Nonsense.

"Would you like to ride in my aeroplane?" he asks.

"N..." Little Miss Wise starts to say.

But then she changes her mind and exclaims:
"Oh, yes please!"

You think she is being very unwise, don't you?
You think she should have learnt her
lesson by now, don't you?

Well she is safe this time.

Because Mr Nonsense's aeroplane
doesn't have any wings,
or an engine,
or even wheels.

It's just a doormat.

Have you ever heard of such nonsense!

3 Great Offers for MR. MEN Fans!

MR. MEN TOKEN

1 New Mr. Men or Little Miss Library Bus Presentation Cases

A brand new stronger, roomier school bus library box, with sturdy carrying handle and stay-closed fasteners.
The full colour, wipe-clean boxes make a great home for your full collection.
They're just £5.99 inc P&P and free bookmark!

☐ MR. MEN   ☐ LITTLE MISS (please tick and order overleaf)

2 Door Hangers and Posters

In every Mr. Men and Little Miss book like this one, you will find a special token. Collect 6 tokens and we will send you a brilliant Mr. Men or Little Miss poster and a Mr. Men or Little Miss double sided full colour bedroom door hanger of your choice. Simply tick your choice in the list and tape a 50p coin for your two items to this page.

PLEASE STICK YOUR 50P COIN HERE

Door Hangers (please tick)
☐ Mr. Nosey & Mr. Muddle
☐ Mr. Slow & Mr. Busy
☐ Mr. Messy & Mr. Quiet
☐ Mr. Perfect & Mr. Forgetful
☐ Little Miss Fun & Little Miss Late
☐ Little Miss Helpful & Little Miss Tidy
☐ Little Miss Busy & Little Miss Brainy
☐ Little Miss Star & Little Miss Fun

Posters (please tick)
☐ MR.MEN
☐ LITTLE MISS

3 Sixteen Beautiful Fridge Magnets – any 2 for £2.00!

inc.P&P

They're very special collector's items!
Simply tick your first and second* choices from the list below
of any 2 characters!

1st Choice

- ☐ Mr. Happy
- ☐ Mr. Lazy
- ☐ Mr. Topsy-Turvy
- ☐ Mr. Bounce
- ☐ Mr. Bump
- ☐ Mr. Small
- ☐ Mr. Snow
- ☐ Mr. Wrong

- ☐ Mr. Daydream
- ☐ Mr. Tickle
- ☐ Mr. Greedy
- ☐ Mr. Funny
- ☐ Little Miss Giggles
- ☐ Little Miss Splendid
- ☐ Little Miss Naughty
- ☐ Little Miss Sunshine

2nd Choice

- ☐ Mr. Happy
- ☐ Mr. Lazy
- ☐ Mr. Topsy-Turvy
- ☐ Mr. Bounce
- ☐ Mr. Bump
- ☐ Mr. Small
- ☐ Mr. Snow
- ☐ Mr. Wrong

- ☐ Mr. Daydream
- ☐ Mr. Tickle
- ☐ Mr. Greedy
- ☐ Mr. Funny
- ☐ Little Miss Giggles
- ☐ Little Miss Splendid
- ☐ Little Miss Naughty
- ☐ Little Miss Sunshine

*Only in case your first choice is out of stock.

--- TO BE COMPLETED BY AN ADULT ---

To apply for any of these great offers, ask an adult to complete the coupon below and send it with
the appropriate payment and tokens, if needed, to MR. MEN CLASSIC OFFER, PO BOX 715, HORSHAM RH12 5WG

☐ Please send _____ Mr. Men Library case(s) and/or _____ Little Miss Library case(s) at £5.99 each inc P&P
☐ Please send a poster and door hanger as selected overleaf. I enclose six tokens plus a 50p coin for P&P
☐ Please send me _____ pair(s) of Mr. Men/Little Miss fridge magnets, as selected above at £2.00 inc P&P

Fan's Name _____

Address _____

_____ **Postcode** _____

Date of Birth _____

Name of Parent/Guardian _____

Total amount enclosed £ _____

☐ **I enclose a cheque/postal order payable to Egmont Books Limited**

☐ **Please charge my MasterCard/Visa/Amex/Switch or Delta account** (delete as appropriate)

Card Number

Expiry date ___/___   **Signature** _____

Please allow 28 days for delivery. Offer is only available while stocks last. We reserve the right to change the terms
of this offer at any time and we offer a 14 day money back guarantee. This does not affect your statutory rights.
Data Protection Act: If you do not wish to receive other similar offers from us or companies we recommend, please
tick this box ☐. Offers apply to UK only.

MR. MEN   LITTLE MISS
Mr. Men and Little Miss™ &©Mrs. Roger Hargreaves